ARTSAKH, STAY STRONG

My name is Angela Asatrian. I'm an Armenian American, born and raised in Glendale, California. I'm a social worker, filmmaker, and writer.
During my Master's in social work at the University of Southern California, I had the opportunity to study human trafficking in the Philippines.
I documented my experience and created a student film highlighting the horrors of the sex trafficking industry.

It was during this time that I realized my true passions: social justice and making films. It is through my films and books that I hope to give a voice to those individuals who may not have the avenue or opportunity to do so.

When the 2020 Nagorno-Karabakh War (or as we Armenians call it, the Artsakh War) started, I didn't understand why Azerbaijan and Turkey had attacked Artsakh. I was enraged by the horrendous acts I heard and saw through social media. I knew I needed to learn more. So, I started doing some research on the history of Armenia and its surrounding regions to better understand why this happened and why the media claimed that this war was over disputed territories.

Chapter 1:
Armenian History

Armenia's history goes back thousands of years to prehistoric times. Armenia has often been regarded by scholars as, "The Cradle of Civilization," where first human settlements began to take place. The Armenian people speak an Indo-European language that is dated around 7,800 BC and is the oldest surviving language in that linguistic family.

If you love shoes and wine, you should know that archaeologists have discovered the world's earliest known wine-making facility and leather shoe near the settlement of Areni in Armenia.
It dates back to 3500 and 4000 BC.

Archaeologists have also discovered many ancient sites across Armenia. They have found artifacts of ancient carpet weaving, pottery making, rock inscriptions, and woodworking. These arts and crafts have been part of the Armenian heritage for millenniums and continue to be a significant part of the culture to this very day.

We all know the story of Noah's Ark from the Bible. But did you know that when the Great Flood took place, it is said that Noah's Ark landed on top of Mount Ararat? Mt. Ararat is located in the heart of ancient Armenia. This would make one wonder if Noah and his descendants settled and rebuilt their lives in Armenia.

The first Armenian kingdoms are mentioned in Mesopotamian and other primary sources as early as the 3rd millennium BC. They were referred to in various ancient sources as Aratta, Armani, Hayasa and Urartu.

The Armenian Kingdoms of Ararat (Urartu) flourished from the second half of the 2nd millennium BC to the 6th century BC and was the rival of ancient Assyria. Urartu was considered as one of the superpowers of the Ancient World.

Artaxiad Dynasty Flag : 189 BC – 1 AD

Arsacid Dynasty Flag : 52 AD – 428 AD

Bagratid Kingdom of Armenia Flag : 885 AD – 1045

Armenian Kingdom of Cilicia Flag : 1198 AD -1219 AD

For the next thousands of years Armenia had many kingdoms, dynasties and empires, such as the Orontid, Artaxiad, Arsacid, Bagratid, Rubenid, Hethumid and Lusignan dynasties.

Artashes The Merciful : Reign : 189 – 160 BC

Levon The Magnificent : Reign : 1198 – 1219 BC

Queen Parandzem : Reign : 350 – 368 BC

Tigran The Great : Reign : 95 – 56 BC

Some of the outstanding Armenian Kings and Queens included Artashes the Merciful, Tigran the Great, Queen Erato, Trdat I, Queen Parandzem, Gagik I, Levon the Magnificent, Queen Zabel and many others.

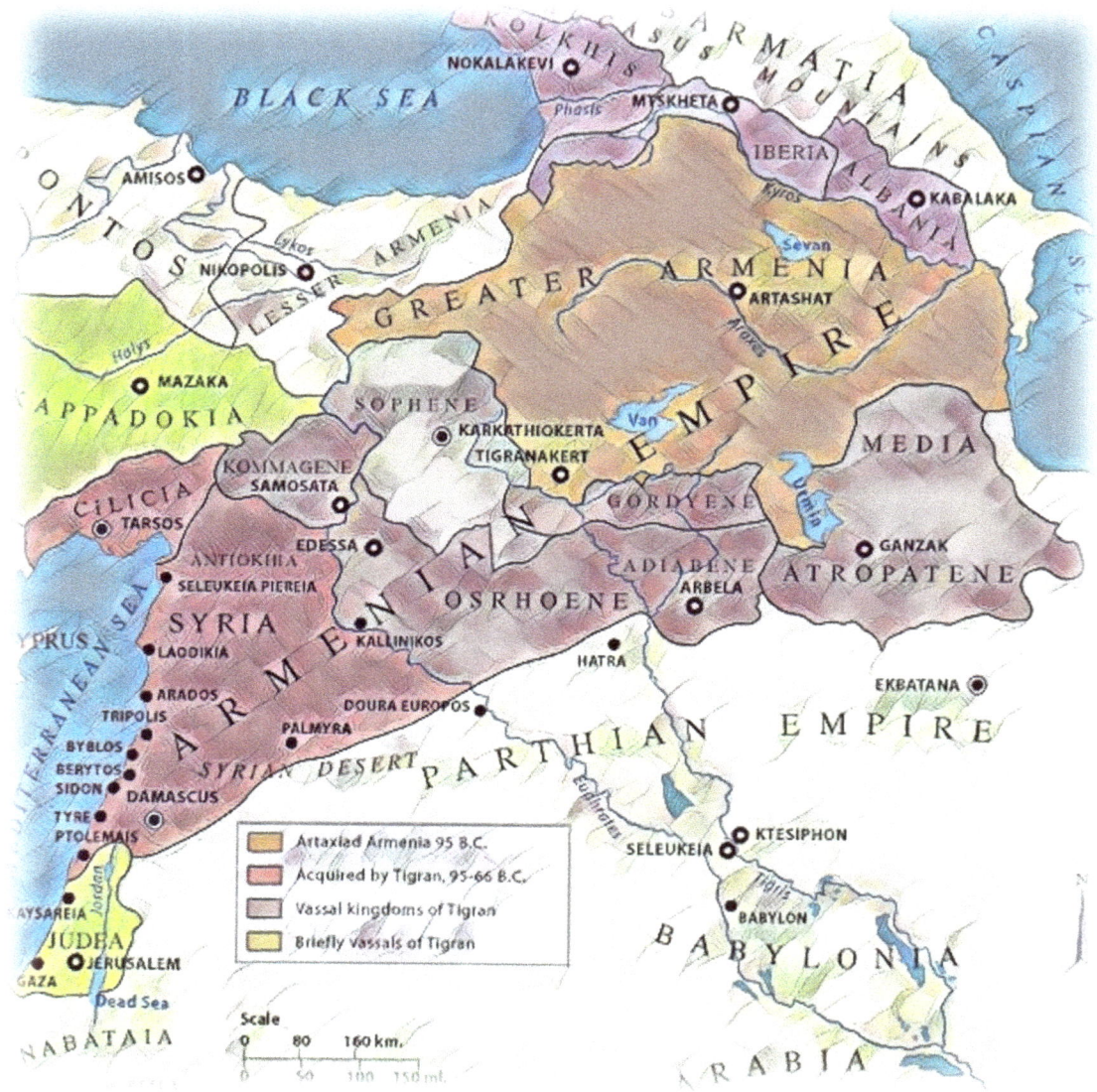

Armenia was territorially at its largest during the reign of Tigran the Great, who built at least 7 cities across Armenia bearing his name – Tigranakert, which in Armenian literally means "built by Tigran." The Classical Greco-Roman authors praised these cities as great cultural centers of the Ancient World.

In 301 AD, Saint Gregory the Illuminator converted the Armenian King Trdat III to Christianity, making Armenia the first nation to adopt Christianity as its state religion.

In 303 AD, the construction of the Armenian Mother Cathedral of Holy Etchmiadzin began. The Holy Etchmiadzin Cathedral became the seat of the Armenian Church.

Ա ա	Բ բ	Գ գ	Դ դ	Ե ե	Զ q	Է է	Ը ը	Թ թ	Ժ ժ
a	b	g	d	je	z	e	ë	t'	ž

Ի ի	Լ լ	Խ խ	Ծ ծ	Կ կ	Հ h	Ձ ձ	Ղ ղ	Ճ ճ	Մ մ
i	l	x	ts	k	h	dz	ṙ	tš	m

Յ յ	Ն ն	Շ շ	Ո ո	Չ չ	Պ պ	Ջ ջ	Ռ ռ	Ս ս	Վ վ
j	n	š	vo	tš'	p	dž	r	s	v

Տ տ	Ր ր	Ց ց	Ւ ւ	Փ փ	Ք ք	Օ o	Ֆ ֆ
t	r'	ts'	w	p'	k'	o	f

In 405 AD, Mesrop Mashtots revived the use of the Armenian alphabet. Several primary sources, such as his pupil Koryun, noted that Mashtots revised an earlier Armenian writing system and modified it for his own alphabet.

After the 5th century, Armenia was divided and under the control of other empires such as the Sassanids of Iran, the Byzantine Empire and the Arab Caliphate. Around the 11th century, nomadic tribes from Central Asia, such as the Seljuk Turks, invaded Armenia. During these times, Armenia lost its independence. However, there were intervals when Armenians liberated themselves and restored their independence.

The Bagratids ruled Armenia until 1045 AD. They established new great cities such as Kars and Ani, which became leading centers of trade, commerce, and culture throughout the medieval world. At its height in the 11th century, Ani was one of the world's largest cities, with a population of more than 100,000. Due to the abundance of its magnificent churches and cathedrals, the city of Ani was dubbed as "the city of 1001 churches."

By the 1500s, Armenia was divided between the Persian Safavid and the Ottoman Turkish empires. These two empires often fought each other, and their main battleground, unfortunately, was Armenia.

In the early 19th century, the expanding Russian Empire took over parts of Eastern Armenia that were previously ruled by the Persian Empire. However, Western Armenia continued to be governed by the Ottomans.

Mekertich Portukalian (1848-1921)

In 1885, the first Armenian political party, the Armenakans, was formed by Mekertich Portukalian in Van, Western Armenia. The party was formed to fight against Turkish oppression. The Armenian Revolutionary Federation was established in 1890 and was instrumental in the defense of Armenia.

From 1894 to 1896, Turkish and Kurdish forces began systematic attacks on Armenians throughout the Ottoman Empire with direct orders from the Ottoman Turkish Sultan Abdul Hamid II. Approximately 300,000 Armenians were killed, and tens of thousands were forced to flee their native homes. This is known as the Hamidian massacres.

In 1908, the Young Turks, also known as the "Committee of Union and Progress," came to power in Turkey. In 1909, the Young Turks massacred some forty thousand Armenians in Adana and other Armenian cities.
These killings are known as the Adana massacre.

However, the epitome of horror by the Young Turks culminated with the Armenian Genocide of 1915 – 1923. During this time, approximately 1.5 million Armenians were slaughtered throughout the Ottoman Empire, including Western Armenia.

To this day, Turkey continues to deny its genocide of the Armenian people. Yet many countries throughout the world, including the United States, have formally recognized the Armenian Genocide and have also condemned Turkey for its continued denial of the atrocities.

In the midst of World War I, as the Armenian Genocide raged throughout much of Armenia, the Armenians fought three heroic self-defense battles in Aparan, Vanadzor, and most importantly, Sardarapat.

The Armenian victories during these battles paved the way for the creation of the fledgling Republic of Armenia, which was declared on May 28, 1918, and only encompassed a very small portion of Armenia. Yerevan became the capital of the new Republic and has remained so until the present day.

In 1919, at the Paris Peace Conference, the victorious Allies, which included the United States, Great Britain, France, Italy, and others, proposed to reestablish a United State of Armenia. This would unite Eastern and Western portions of Armenia into a single Armenian State and would encompass a territory of around 125,000 square miles. The Allies explained that the creation of a United Armenia was the just restitution to the Armenian people who had survived the Genocide implemented by the Turkish government.

On August 10, 1920, the Republic of Armenia became a signatory of the Treaty of Sevres, by which Turkey recognized Armenia as a free, independent, and united country. On November 22, 1920, President Woodrow Wilson made his famous Arbitral Award, which established the international border between Armenia and Turkey.

Mustafa Kemal Ataturk

Vladimir Ilyich Ulyanov aka Lenin

However, the Turkish ultra-nationalist leader, Mustafa Kemal, ignored the new treaty and attacked Armenia, and occupied the Armenian cities of Kars and Alexandropol (Gyumri). Kemal and the Bolshevik leader, Lenin, made an infamous alliance, which resulted in an invasion, occupation, and partition of Armenia by the Turks and Bolsheviks.

In late 1920, what remained of the Republic of Armenia was proclaimed as a Soviet Republic. The United States government and the European Allies condemned this act of aggression and never recognized the occupation and partition of the Republic of Armenia by the Kemalists and the Bolsheviks.

In the early 1920s, Soviet dictator Josef Stalin, who succeeded Lenin, forcefully made the Armenian regions of Nakhichevan and Artsakh part of Soviet Azerbaijan. The Armenians of Artsakh, who made up more than 90% of the population of this Armenian province, never accepted this unjust and unlawful decision.

In 1988, after many decades of occupation, the Armenian people began a wave of democratic protests, which called for the just return of the majority Armenian populated region of Artsakh to Armenia. However, the Soviet Azeri leaders rejected this democratic movement and launched a series of massacres of Armenians throughout Azerbaijan and Artsakh.
They also began a blockage of Armenian fuel supply lines.

List of Armenian Massacres

Name	Date	Location	Perpetrators	Armenian Victims
Hamidian Massacres	1894-1896	Ottoman Empire	Ottoman Government	88,243-300,000
Adana Massacre	April 1909	Adana	Anti- Armenian Mobs	19,479-25,000
Armenian Genocide	1915-1922	Ottoman Empire	Committee of Union and Progress (Young Turks)	800,000-1,500,000
September Days	September 1918	Azerbaijan	Azeri-Turkish Authorities	10,000-30,000
Agulis Massacre	December 25-25, 1919	Agulis, Armenia	Azeri-Turkish Authorities	1,400
Khaibalikend Massacre	June 1919	Karabakh-Artsakh	Azeri Army	700
Shushi Massacre	March 1920	Shushi	Azeri Army	500-20,000
Turkish-Armenian War	September-December 1920	Armenia	Turkish National Forces	60,000-198,000
Sumgait Pogrom	February 1988	Sumgait, Azerbaijan	Azeri Mobs	26-200
Kirovabad Pogrom	November 1988	Kirovobad, Azerbaijan	Azeri Mobs	10-130
Baku Pogrom	January 1990	Baku, Azerbaijan	Azeri Mobs	90
Maraga Massacre	April 10, 1992	Maraga, Karabakh	Azeri Armed Forces	50-100

On September 2, 1991, Artsakh declared its independence, using its lawful right as an Autonomous Region within the USSR. A few weeks later, Armenia followed in its footsteps. Armenia joined the United Nations on March 2, 1992, and its first elected President was Levon Ter-Petrossian.

Monte Melkonian (1957-1993), Armenian-American Revolutionary.

After the reestablishment of a Free Armenia, the Armenian people faced serious challenges from neighboring Azerbaijan and Turkey. The Azeris rejected Artsakh's declaration of independence and, in 1991 launched an all-out invasion. A bloody war from 1991 to 1994 took thousands of lives on both sides. By 1994, the Armenians were able to defend their land, and a ceasefire was signed in May. This effectively ended major fighting until April of 2016, when the Azeris launched a new aggression against Artsakh.

In September of 2020, Azeri dictator Ilham Aliyev, supported by The Turkish Army, including the Turkish Air Force and thousands of mercenary jihadi terrorists recruited from Syria, launched an all-out invasion on Artsakh. After 44 days of war, the Azeris were able to occupy much of Artsakh, including its historic Armenian town of Shushi.

The war ended on November 10, 2020 and lasted for 44 days. It killed approximately 4,000 Armenian soldiers and 400 civilians. For a county with a population of about three million, those numbers are staggering.

Garnik Khlghatyan (2001-2020)

One of the soldiers killed was my cousin, Garnik. He was born on July 28, 2001 and was killed on September 27, 2020. He was only 19 years old. My Uncle Ashot, who is in his 60s, had also volunteered to fight during the war. He continues to serve to this day.

BREAKING NEWS

NEWS LIVE

CORONAVIRUS PANDEMIC

This war occurred during the height of the pandemic when the entire world was shut down and battling the spread of COVID 19. Azerbaijan pounced on the opportunity to attack. I couldn't just sit by and watch another genocide take place. I knew I had to do something.

I found The Center for Truth and Justice (CFTJ), a nonprofit organization comprised of attorneys from the diaspora. They are gathering testimonies from soldiers, prisoners of war (POWs), and displaced people to provide evidence for international court.

I told them about my project, and they agreed to let me join them. I packed my bags and flew to Armenia with a few members of the organization.

Our secret escape: Shorzha Beach at Lake Sevan.

My favorite Monastery, Geghard.

Sardarapat Memorial is a must see.

My favorite restaurant to eat fish, Lcher.

Mother Armenia statue in Yerevan.

I met with Anahit Harutyunyan and Arsineh Arakel, members of CFTJ. We got to work right away and started gathering testimonies. We drove all over Armenia, interviewing POWs, displaced individuals, historians, and others. I helped them with filming, and they helped connect me to the right people for my project.

49

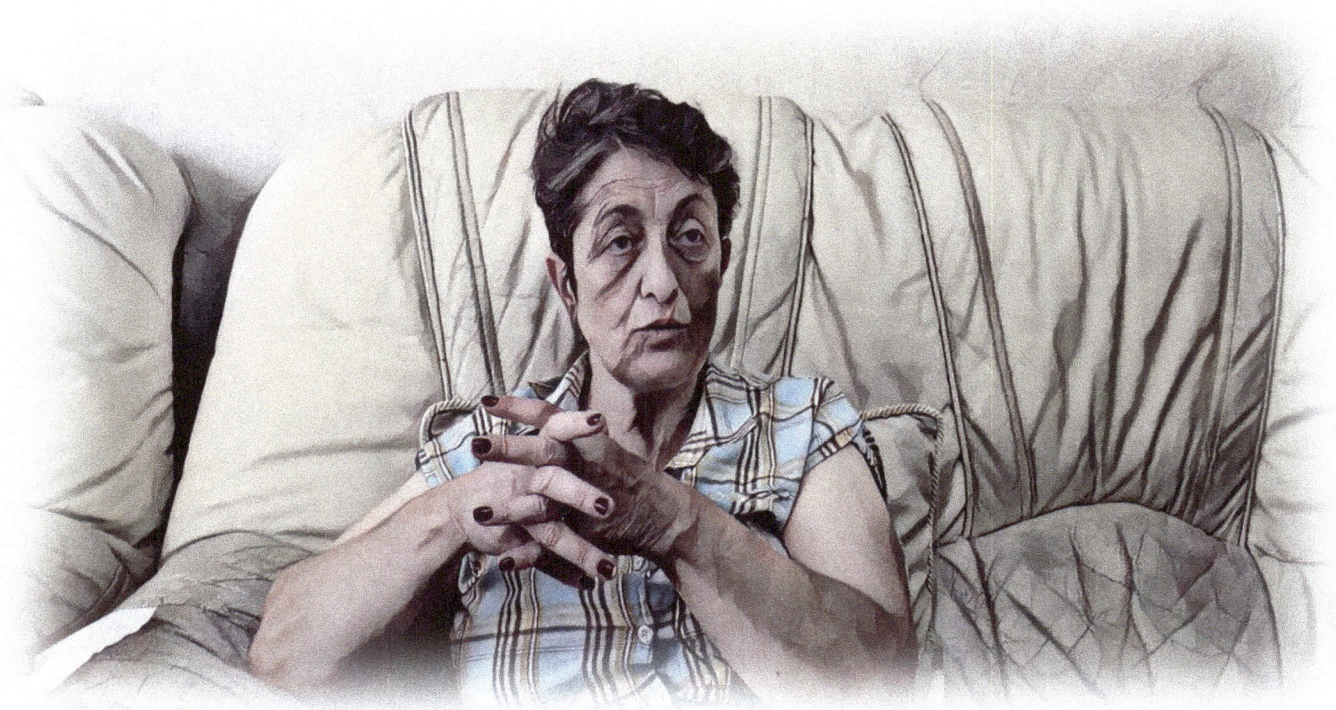

We met with this woman whose name will not be mentioned. She is a local from Hadrut (a village in Artsakh/Nagorno-Karabakh) who lost her home during the war. She invited us into her temporary housing and shared her story with us. "The war of 2020 started very suddenly. On the morning of September 27th, we were at home, asleep, and all of a sudden, the bombing started. My husband told me to take the kids to a bomb shelter quickly. Afterward, the Bayraktar drones came and started bombing Hadrut. There was shelling in the residential areas. They had bombed right in our yard. I was kneeling down, and a piece of shrapnel barely missed me. So it was then that we realized this was a different type of war that was starting."

"I had never left Hadrut during any war. My husband worked there. They had already enlisted my son. I couldn't leave. I thought that if I left Artsakh, it would be as if I'm abandoning a sick parent who is bedridden. That's how I felt. My husband came home and told me I had to leave Hadrut. I told him, 'I can't leave you. Where would I go? You're here. Where would I go?' He replied, 'You have to leave this time. This isn't 1992.' So I left and went to Azokh, where they relocated the Hadrut hospital."

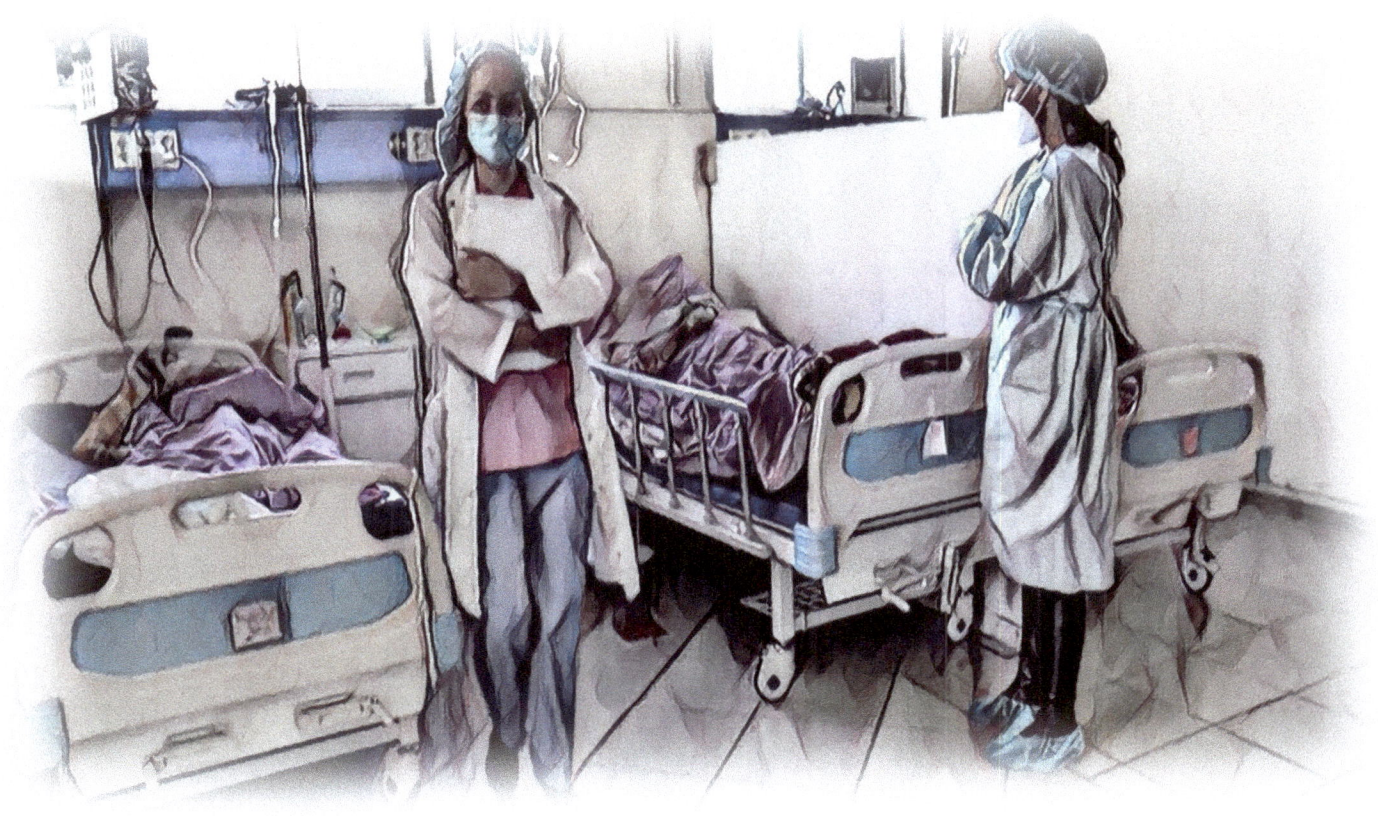

"I went and saw that there was no space there. They had just relocated. They had no water, and no proper conditions. The hospital was new. They still had to set up the operating beds. Everything was a mess. But those first couple days that I was in Hadrut, until the 3rd or 4th, I went to the hospital every day because I was always afraid that they would bring in one of my family members... At least I could be there to take care of them," she said as she teared up.

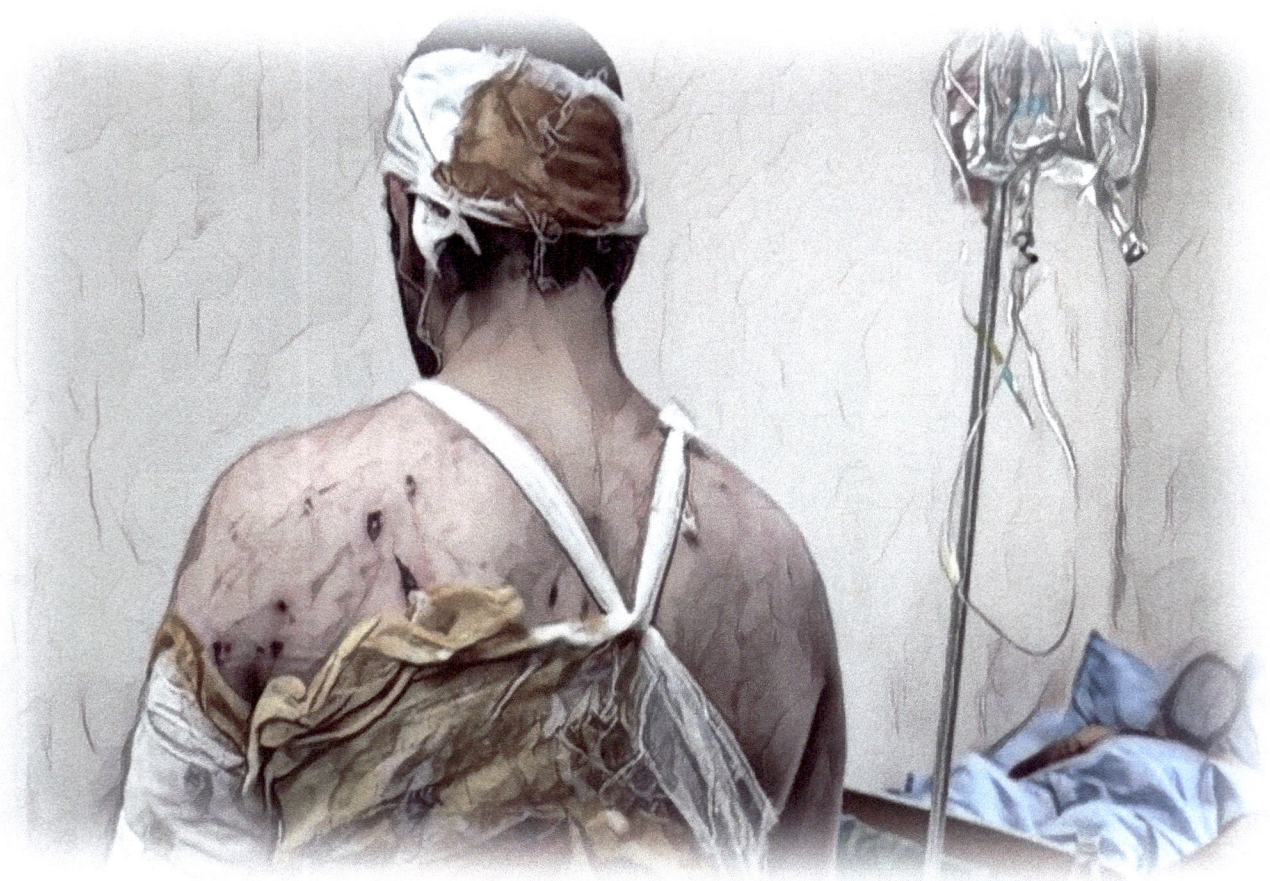

"In 1992, when they brought in the corpses and the wounded, you could tell that they were simply wounded. They were shot, and they were wounded. This time, I don't know, how do I explain this to you? When they would bring in people, their whole body was covered in small perforations from those blasts. The UAVs would hover above as if they were teasing you. It would spin and spin and spin and then explode in the air, and all the shrapnel would rain down on you."

"And one day, I will never forget this. Their bodies were deformed as if they were pieces of paper that had been crumpled. I don't know what kind of weapons those were, and then the boys said that it was a TOS Solntsepyok. They had fired at our boys with that TOS Solntsepyok. Half of them were burned, half of them were injured like I described, the rest were just remnants of a human body, mixed with the dirt."

She continued to discuss the war, which led to us talking about the 1990s movement known as the Karabakh movement. "It was incomprehensible for us. We had a population of 150,000, going up against 7 to 8 million Azerbaijanis. We resisted. We fought. We conducted our national liberation movement according to all international laws. But for a reason which is unknown, the world did not recognize us. Not our movement, not our wars, not our resistance for 30 years."

"I think it is because we are a hindrance here. Yes, it's true. We're a hindrance to Turkey. We bother Turkey a lot because their plan is to create a Pan-Turkey, and we are what stands in the way of that plan." We thanked her for her time and for sharing her story with us and continued our journey.

I've heard of Pan-Turkism before, but I thought that was a thing of the past... during the Ottoman era and the Armenian Genocide. Armenia is located between Turkey and Azerbaijan... by taking over Armenia or a portion of it, it would connect Turkey to its brother country, Azerbaijan, and then connect to the rest of the Turkic nations. It made me wonder if there's more to this war than disputed territories.

Chapter 2: Pan-Turkism

I started doing some research on Pan-Turkism and came across a handful of videos of both Turkish President Recep Tayyip Erdogan and Azerbaijani President Ilham Aliyev. In this video, President Erdogan stated, "We will continue to fulfill this mission, which our grandfathers have carried out for centuries, in the Caucasus again. Turkey will not hesitate to side with Azerbaijan, a country that has a long friendship and brotherly relations, against any attack to its right and territory."

In this video, President of Azerbaijan Ilham Aliyev said, "Over the past 18 years, both Turkey and Azerbaijan have formed a common policy. Before that, in my father's time, he made this famous statement, 'One nation, two states.' These words are a guiding light for us. True to this testament and these words, we have strengthened our relations in all directions, elevated them to a higher standard."

I began to feel a bit fearful. Could Erdogan and Aliyev be working towards Pan-Turkic expansionism? I needed to learn more, so I met with a handful of individuals experienced in the subject.

The first person I met was Turkish journalist Uzay Bulut. We met over Zoom as she is currently in hiding. I asked her about her thoughts on Pan-Turkism, and this was her response, "Pan-Turkish ideology, which aims to unite the Turkic world, also targets Armenia because they see Armenia as an obstacle for their Pan-Turkic goals. For example, right now, they are trying to build a corridor. They are trying to extend the Azeri expansionism in Armenia, and by 2023, I think they will take another step towards that goal."

I then met Missiologist Jacob Pursley. He's an American Christian Minister that lived in Turkey for about 15 years ministering and then moved to Armenia in 2017. We discussed Pan-Turkism, and he shared, "Since the time of Mohammad until 1923, there has been a succession of caliphates until Sultan Ahmed. And Ataturk, the founder of the Republic of Turkey disbanded the caliphate. So now they've been this secular, democratic republic since 1923, and Erdogan, is saying we are going to change things in 2023, and this is our plan."

THE ZANGAZUR CORRIDOR IS A PROJECT THAT CAN UNITE THE TURKIC WORLD,

He continued saying, "Part of that plan is to return to a Neo-Ottoman Turkic Empire going back to the way it used to be. They want to connect the Turkic region in Azerbaijan, northern Iran, with the Azeris living there, Turkmenistan, Nakhichevan, Uzbekistan, just name all the stans that are Turkic, and he wants to unite them. But his goal for this year, he's made it very clear, is 2023."

Fatma Muge Gocek is a Turkish Sociologist who was born and raised in Turkey. She has written many books, including, <u>Denial of Violence: Ottoman Past, Turkish Present, and Collective Violence Against Armenians</u>. I wanted to get her opinion on this war and her thoughts on Pan-Turkism. I asked her if she thought Pan-Turkism could be one of the reasons behind the war, and she responded, "It's not one of the reasons... I'd say the fundamental reason behind this war is definitely Pan-Turkism. It has nothing to do with the Azeris living there and who they are. The idea is expanding in that direction."

She continued to say, "What is sad about Pan-Turkism is that it is still in existence today, and the fact that they deny the Armenian Genocide to this day means that they never came to terms with their nationalism, unfortunately." I do have to admit; it was a bit of a struggle for me to meet with and talk to a Turk, given our history. But knowing her ideals made it much easier for me. The experience was a friendly reminder that not all Turks are hateful and extremists. I thanked her for sharing her knowledge and expertise with me, and we ended the meeting with a hug.

I then watched hours of The International Court of Justice Court Hearing of Armenia vs. Azerbaijan, in which Professor Pierre D'Argent, an International Law Expert, stated, "In late March of 2021, Azerbaijan destroyed the monument commemorating the Genocide implemented by the Ottoman Empire. Denying the Genocide, the defendant feels he is entitled to destroy this monument because it commemorates an event that, according to him, did not occur. There could not be a stronger symbol that President Aliyev making of the rewriting of history a social point in his ethnic-nationalistic discriminatory policy. There is no place, no room in the territories controlled by Azerbaijan for what makes and symbolizes Armenian identity."

Turkey and Azerbaijan continue to deny the Armenian Genocide. The Treaty of Sevres and Woodrow Wilson's Arbitral Award was supposed to provide justice and restitution to the survivors of the Armenian Genocide. Why didn't we get those lands back? I needed answers, so I met with Mr. Ara Papian, an Armenian lawyer, historian, and diplomat who is an expert in this subject.

I asked Mr. Papian if he could discuss more about the treaty and why Armenia never got those lands back, and he stated, "The Treaty of Sevres is a Peace Treaty signed between the defeated Ottoman Empire and the victorious powers, among them, the Republic of Armenia. And according to article 89, the title and right of former Ottoman vilayets, Van, Bitlis, Trabzon, and Erzurum, went to Armenia, which means that that became part of the Armenian State. Unfortunately, when that deal was signed and sealed by the great seal of the U.S.A. on November 22, 1920, it never was implemented because Kemal Ataturk received great support by the Russian Bolsheviks, ignored the arbitral award, defeated the Armenian State, and forced everybody to recognize his unlawful rights.

He continued to say, "Nowadays, we see that the relationship between the U.S. and Turkey are worsening, and we hope that because of this, the Armenian question will rise once more, and the Arbitral Award will be the main leverage over Turkey." I asked him if the Arbitral Award is still valid as it has been over 100 years since it was signed, and he replied, "Yes, because, according to the Hague Convention of 1889, Article 54, if the award is done and given to the representative of the parties, it enters and has no time limitation and is final."

Wow! I couldn't believe that the Arbitral Award is still valid. So legally, those lands should belong to the Armenians. Why isn't anyone fighting for this? Sadly, I can't imagine any country trying to force President Erdogan to do anything he doesn't want to do. After all, Turkey is a member of NATO and is an important U.S. security partner. Well, a girl could dream.

I went home and dreamt of Western Armenia reuniting with Eastern Armenia when I came across this video of Aliyev stating, "I do hope that Armenia, which has been defeated, because of its policy of aggression, will sooner or later realize that its territorial claims to any country will not bring them good or honor. I do hope that Armenians' territorial claims to both Turkey and Azerbaijan will end in the near future. Otherwise, they may find themselves in an even more precarious situation." Boy, did that boil my blood.

While President Aliyev threatens the Armenian government to relinquish any territorial claims, Azerbaijan continues to make multiple encroachments onto Armenian territory (2020, 2021, and 2022, post trilateral statement). Sadly, Azerbaijan continues to hold Armenian POWs in custody and uses them as bargaining chips to gain leverage.

A video was leaked of President Erdogan, First Lady Mrs. Erdogan, and President Aliyev on a bus discussing the return of Armenian POWs in exchange for minefield maps. President Aliyev stated, "If we get all the minefield maps, we will have a great advantage because it may take ten years to clear these areas." In which Mrs. Erdogan asks, "Do you still have more prisoners of war?" and President Aliyev replies, "Yes, yes, of course, a lot," and Mrs. Erodgan's shocking response to that comment was, "Return them, little by little."

I met with Mr. David Phillips, Director of the Peacebuilding and Human Rights program at Columbia University. We discussed the POW situation, and he shared, "I've seen a list of ethnic Armenians that are being detained. These are POWs. The list includes 170 people. There may be more that don't appear on the list, but clearly they're pawns in a larger geopolitical conflict, and according to the Geneva Convention and international law, they can't be held. They must be released."

I wanted to hear more stories from those affected by the war. I was introduced to Tigran and his family. They agreed to share their story with me. So we hopped in the car and drove to Gyumri to meet with them and hear about their experience.

This is Tigran's Grandmother, Hasmik. She shared her story first, "My grandson Mels (Tigran's brother) was very empathetic, very modest, very personable, hard-working. He respected his elders. He was a precious boy. What is there to say? This accursed war threw this whole family into chaos. I praise the Lord... we have faith in the will of the Lord, in the will of good people, that our child returns. That everyone's child returns. Let no mother mourn; let no mother and daughter weep. I am also a mother. I see how their actions torture her. It tortures me too."

"I have four grandchildren, but out of all them, my Mels is special. We had the strongest connection. The last time he called me, we spoke; I asked him, 'My darling, won't you come home?' and he said, 'Grandma dear, tomorrow I'm already heading out.' We did not know anything. We thought that with the Russians here, the war had stopped, and in sixteen days, he would return. But this is how things are. Hope is all we have to bear us. May all the mothers have patience, and may this country see peace. By the will of God, these problems will end."

Tigran and Mels' Mom, Nelli, shares, "My other son, Tigran, was already fighting in the war so Mels didn't get drafted. But he felt guilty, and he wanted to go and fight. He told me, 'No. I will go and fight and stand at my brother's side.' We told him that if he went, he wouldn't be guaranteed to be stationed by his brother. And he told me, 'They'll station me with someone's brother, and someone's brother will stand with mine. We will win, arm-in-arm.'"

"Then one day, he came home and said, 'They've called me to fight.' We knew they didn't call him as his brother was already there, but I did nothing. I knew how he was feeling. He couldn't just sit by and watch while his country was in turmoil. So he packed his things and left. When the war had stopped, he called me saying, 'Mom, they're rotating us out, so I'll be home tomorrow.' Tomorrow came, and he did not return. We called him, but no one answered. We could not reach him. On November 13, we found out he was taken as a POW."

"Since his capture, we've only received a few letters from him. In his letters, he was so apologetic, he wrote, 'Mother, forgive me for not listening to you. I will be good. I won't do anything wrong so I can come back. I will come back. Just don't cry and be strong.' I am so proud to have sons like these. Selfless boys. Both of them would give their lives for their country. They stand with their country. I suffer every day knowing my child right now is away from me. But I have hope, hope for his return."

We interviewed more families, but they wished for me not to share their stories. These interviews crushed me; I was so heartbroken. So many families have lost their children to this war from both sides, and for what? Territorial gains? Profit? Pan-Turkism doesn't just affect Armenia. Turkey has attacked the Greeks, Syrians, Kurds, and others. Their expansion and goals could soon become a threat to other countries as well. I pray that no other nation goes through what we have gone through and continue to go through.

So many families like Mel's family anxiously wait and hope that our prisoners of war are returned. We know that they are using our POWs as pawns for political gain, but that doesn't explain why they are torturing and beheading our soldiers and destroying our cultural sites. It makes me think that Pan-Turkism isn't the only driving force behind this war.

Chapter 3: Armenophobia

Mr. David Phillips and I discussed more about the war, and he told me, "This war is not about territory in my mind. It's about racism and hatred of Armenians... so it's possible for individuals to feel hate towards one another, but when hatred becomes institutionalized, when it becomes government policy, it's really hard to turn around. Since the 1990s until today and since the recent war in Artsakh, Azerbaijan has made an industry out of hating and demonizing Armenians. It's going to be very hard to move forward from this point."

Ilham Aliyev ✔
@presidentaz

· · ·

Armenia is not even a colony, it is not even worthy of being a servant.

12:37 AM · Jan 29, 2015 · Twitter Web Client

I continued to watch the International Court of Justice hearings to gather more information. In this hearing, Mr. Lawrence Martin, an International Law expert stated, "President Aliyev, who inherited the job from his father and has held the highest position in the land for 18 years, continues to spew racist hatred to this day. As recently as last month, he said Armenians have 'a mental illness' and called them worse than animals and 'a deprived tribe.'"

President Aliyev walks past a display of helmets worn by martyred Armenian soldiers at Trophy Park.

Wax mannequins of Armenian soldiers chained in their cells, located at Trophy Park.

Throughout the war, I came across multiple videos of Eric Hacopian. He's a political analyst and was covering the conflict. I knew I had to talk to him. I met with him at his office, and he shared his thoughts with me. "There has always been hatred of Armenians in Azerbaijan; however, systematic hatred of Armenians began about 30 years ago. Azerbaijan is a nation that has no history and no culture, so they built their identity based on a negative identity, on hatred of the other and the other, in this case, is Armenians. Their national identity is based on the hatred of Armenians. They even created this hideous park in Baku called Trophy Park, which is literally, if you look at the imagery, its Nazi-like. Flat-headed Armenians with big noses... these are Nazi imagery."

"The official stamps of the state are about exterminating Armenians; someone putting pesticide on Artsakh. The national hero of Azerbaijan is an ax murderer. I don't even want to name him, but this guy; he goes off and murders someone who is sleeping. This act shows what a coward he is. It's an act of a coward."

"He receives a life sentence, but the Hungarian government, which is exceptionally corrupt, accepts the Azeri government's bribes to have him transferred to Azerbaijan to serve out the rest of his sentence. His plane lands, he arrives in Azerbaijan and is greeted as a national hero. He's given a pension, he's given an apartment, he's given a raise, and he's given a higher position. Do we need to say more about the nature of that society and the nature of that state?"

In another International Court of Justice hearing, Professor D'Argent shared some of the destruction in Shushi by Azerbaijan. He stated, "The Cathedral of Shushi was coldly and deliberately pounded twice on the same day so that the deadly message sent was perfectly clear. The Armenians have no place here in Nagorno Karabakh and will never be in security there, not even in their most sacred spaces... since then, Azerbaijan removed the spire of the church, stating that they are returning it to its original architectural form."

He continued to say, "However, if you look at pictures of the church before the 1900s, you will see that the Church's original form had the spire. It was built in 1886 and 1887 when it was part of the Russian Empire. In March 1920, there were Armenian pogroms to ethnically cleanse the city... the spire was then removed. The cathedral resumed its spire in 1998 until it was bombed in 2021. Azerbaijan reveals its policy of racial discrimination after bombing the Armenian cultural heritage... Azerbaijan is altering, modifying what remains of it in order to diminish its presence."

In a BBC interview, the journalist asked President Aliyev, "We have had an attack in Nagorno Karabakh, a Church which has been shelled twice in the same day. Now you have said that possibly it was a mistake and that you would carry out an investigation. What is the result of that investigation?" He replied, "In order to investigate it, we have to be there, to investigate. I said many times, either it was a mistake by our artillery, or it was a deliberate provocation from Armenians themselves."

The journalist asked him, "So you may have done it?" Aliyev replied, "Who you? Who you mean you?" She asked calmly, "Your forces may have done it?" Aliyev shrugged his shoulders and replied, "It could have been by mistake, only because there was no military target; church was not amongst military targets." The journalist cut him off, "But could you have made a mistake twice on the same day? It was hit twice." and Aliyev replied, "Why not?"

In another International Court of Justice hearing, I learned about more destruction from Azerbaijan. Mr. Martin stated, "In an ongoing campaign to erase Armenian presence from its territory just by way of example as revolting as it is, satellite images show on 18th of June 2021, a historic Armenian cemetery was erased for the construction of a road. Azerbaijan is literally paving over Armenian history."

Throughout the war, I saw videos of Arthur Khachents on social media. He's a native of Hadrut, a village in Artsakh, he is also an artist, and a volunteer soldier. While out on duty, Khachents would sing for his fellow soldiers in order to lift their spirits and his own. These videos went viral. I wanted to meet him and hear his stories of the war. I asked him about the cultural destruction, and he replied, "In reality, those lands were ours, not 30 years ago, not 100 years ago, but since the very beginning. That's why there is so much evidence there, like the cross-stones not only above the ground but beneath it."

He continued to say, "They can see that Armenians resided there for thousands of years and that the Armenian culture has a presence there. But as long as there are cross-stones and churches, Turkey does Azerbaijan's dirty work and annihilates any trace of them. They do this either by destruction or by converting them into mosques or Udi churches." This isn't the first time I had heard of Azeris claiming that Armenian churches belong to the Caucasian Albanians or the Udis. I wanted to learn more about this subject.

I met Rouben Galichian, a cartographer and researcher specializing in historical maps. I asked him about the history of Azerbaijan, Caucasian Albanians, and Udis and how those rumors all came about. He stated, "When the Republic of Azerbaijan was established in 1918, in a region that used to be called Shirvan and previously would consist of the Muslim Khanates and before that it was the Caucasian Albanians."

"They were instructed by the central authorities of the communist party; Stalin had decided that each of the republics should have their own individual history and culture. So, imagine a country that has only been established since 1918, and before that, it was a group of various nationals speaking a bunch of different languages. There was no country called Azerbaijan north of the Arax River, and now there is one, and it has to have its own history and culture."

"So, what do you do? The first thing to do is to claim that any foreigner living in that area that is not Azerbaijani is a newcomer. Armenians were called newcomers, stating that they came to that area in 1828, whereas all old historic maps and travel logs show that Armenians have been there for centuries. Now, the second thing to do is whatever there is culturally speaking in that region belongs to the newly established country, to their culture."

"However, this is problematic because the old historical monuments were mainly Christian and had Armenian inscriptions on them. So, what the Azerbaijan authorities did in order to appropriate these monuments, was first to erase the Armenian language inscriptions on them and then announce to the world that this belongs to the Caucasian Albanians. Well, these churches were built mainly between the 9th and 16th centuries and during that time, all Albanians except for a few thousand Udis had converted to Islam. How could Muslims build Armenian churches, Christian monasteries, and khachkars (cross stones)? And if there are monuments that you are unable to appropriate or call them your own, they simply destroy them."

In another International Court of Justice hearing, Professor D'Argent talked about the destruction of Armenian khachkars in Julfa. He stated, "Azerbaijan is accustomed to cultural destruction when it comes to a matter of attacking the Armenian historical culture in Nakhichevan located in the southwest of Armenia. Azerbaijan has committed innumerable cultural destructions especially in 2005; Baku erased literally the oldest cemetery in Julfa, which had thousands of khachkars, the greatest and largest in the world. This was duly documented the worst cultural genocide of the 21st century."

"The response of the authorities in Baku was to try to attempt to change reality, so from historical revisions to negationism, there is only 1 step that Azerbaijan blithely takes through its ambassador in London, whom I quote, 'first and foremost, we need to make it clear that there is no such thing as 'Armenian heritage' in the Nakhchivan Autonomous Republic simply because Armenians never lived there. Non-existing sites or cemeteries cannot be destroyed.'"

Armenians were able to save some khachkars from Shushi before Azerbaijan took over as we knew they would destroy them. They are trying to erase us from these lands in order to claim that it is theirs. Aliyev even made this speech a couple of years ago, "I must also note that we must not forget and do not forget our historical lands. This should become a guideline for our future activities, just as we are working in this direction today."

Erdogan is an enemy to the West

Those lobbyists hardly name any reason why one should support Erdogan despite his current politics. They simply give one reason: "Turkey is important and has to stay in NATO by all means."

By KAMAL SIDO   Published: NOVEMBER 15, 2019 16:54

Turkish President Reçep Tayyip Erdoğan
(photo credit: CEM OKSUZ/TURKISH PRESIDENTIAL PRESS OFFICE/HANDOUT VIA REUTERS)

"Our historical lands are the Irevan khanate, Zangezur, Goycha. Because Irevan is our historical land and we Azerbaijanis must return to these historical lands. This is our political and strategic goal, and we must gradually move closer to it." Wow, now they're trying to say that Yerevan is their historical land? This is terrifying! If the world doesn't wake up, Azerbaijan and Turkey will destroy Armenia. They will unite and make their way toward Europe and the rest of the world.

Chapter 4: War Crimes

Throughout this war, Azerbaijani soldiers posted many videos online showing them torturing and executing Armenian soldiers. I was mortified. I spoke with Ms. Bulut about the war crimes, and she said, "The Azeris are proud of their crimes, both the government and much of the public, because they didn't even feel the need to hide those crimes during the war. They filmed beheadings and showed them on social media. They are proud, and they are unapologetic."

Mr. Phillips told me, "So the war in Artsakh involved a number of different parties. You had the Azerbaijan armed forces, but most of the front-line fighting was done by mercenaries who had been sent to Artsakh from Syria and Libya by Turkey."

Jacob Pursley also shared his thoughts on the war crimes that took place. He stated, "The Turkish government hired mercenaries, Islamic terrorists, to come and fight for Azerbaijan against Artsakh and Armenia... the Armenian government captured some of these mercenaries, and they testified."

A Syrian mercenaries' testimony: "My name is Yousef Abef Elhajji. I'm from the Jisr Shughur region, Zeidiye village (Syria)." The investigator asked Yousef, "What were you promised in exchange for coming here?" He replied, "They promised us $2,000 a month. They said they'd pay our salaries on a monthly basis." The investor asked Yousef if they've come here to fight, and he replied, "Yes, we came here to cut the heads of kaffirs (non-believers) off." The investigator then asked if Yousef was promised any bonus payments, in which he responded, "They said they would watch how we fought... we could get more based on what we did... we would get an extra hundred dollars for the head of each kaffir we cut off."

In an interview with Aljazeera, the journalist said to President Aliyev, "Armenia also accuses Turkey for transferring Syrian opposition fighters to Azerbaijan." He replied, shrewdly, "This is fake news, absolutely." She stated that Armenia has evidence of this, and he responds, "Let them show it. Where is the evidence? Let him give us evidence. Let him give us proof. He uses only words. We can also say many words, but we don't. We behave in a responsible way. There is not a single evidence of any foreign presence in Azerbaijan. If anyone comes from outside to fight as a mercenary, that should be internationally addressed. We reject them, and we demand the evidence be put on the table."

Armenia Provided Data on 250 Mercenaries Deployed by Azerbaijan

by Asbarez Staff — March 4, 2022 — in Armenia, Artsakh, Featured Story, Latest, News, Top Stories   💬 0

The Syrian mercenaries used as 'cannon fodder' in Nagorno-Karabakh

By Ed Butler
BBC News

🕐 10 December 2020

 Nagorno-Karabakh conflict

Syrian mercenaries offer new testimonies from Karabakh war

December 13, 2021 - 17:06 AMT

PanARMENIAN.Net - Syrian mercenaries recruited by Turkey and Azerbaijan to fight against the Armenians of Artsakh (Nagorno-Karabakh) have raised the fact that Baku has not paid them for their "work", over one year after the completion of hostilities.

According to a reportage from the Public TV of Armenia, part of those deployed in the region were used as cannon fodder while those who managed to survive have not been paid.

"We fought with the Turkish state in Karabakh. We have people who were injured and people who were killed. Sultan Suleiman Shah, Abo Amsha stole our rights, and stole the salaries of the injured and dead, and people are dying from hunger," one mercenary is filmed saying.

The Washington Post
Democracy Dies in Darkness

Turkey has denied sending Syrian fighters to aid Azerbaijan, its longtime ally. But relatives of two fighters — Najjar and his nephew — said in interviews that monthly salaries were promised by the Turkish-supported militias and that the fighters flew to Azerbaijan from southern Turkey.

In recent months, Turkey has sought to project its military might across much of its neighborhood with new vigor. Turkey's enthusiastic backing of the Azerbaijani war effort — and provision of military assistance, including armed drones — has emboldened Azerbaijan, situating Turkey at the center of the conflict and giving Ankara standing, it hopes, to weigh in on any peace settlement.

Mahmoud Najjar was a Syrian mercenary who was killed fighting in Nagorno-Karabakh. (Family photo)

Syrians Make Up Turkey's Proxy Army in Nagorno-Karabakh

After fighting Turkey's battles in Libya, the Syrian National Army is caught in the conflict between Armenia and Azerbaijan—and dozens are dying.

By Liz Cookman, a freelance journalist based in Istanbul covering Turkey, Syria, and the wider Middle East.

Okay, President Aliyev, you'd like the evidence? Take a look! Just Google it. There are video testimonies and articles from all sorts of news outlets, not just Armenian. However, I feel you will say that it is fake news.

I talked some more with Mr. Phillips about the crimes that occurred during the war. He stated, "Columbia University has compiled the Artsakh atrocities website, and we've documented extensively the collusion between Azerbaijan, Turkey, and these Islamic mercenaries. And there needs to be accountability." I asked him if there has been any accountability so far, and he replied, "So accountability requires the country where the crime occurred to prosecute the perpetrators. I think there is no chance that Azerbaijan is going to hold its forces accountable. So there needs to be some sort of international mechanism that's established in order to proceed with trials. But the first and most important thing is to document and to preserve evidence of war crimes and crimes against humanity."

Documenting and preserving evidence? That sounds familiar! Oh yes, that's what the Center for Truth and Justice has been doing. At one of the lectures, the Honorable Judge Gassia Apkarian shared with the class, "In order to be able to defend our cause, and no matter where it is and what's happening... it doesn't matter where a conflict is taking place... it doesn't matter what the violation is, you have to collect firsthand evidence... with the work we've done here, we've gathered 75 testimonies, in a matter of 4 to 5 months."

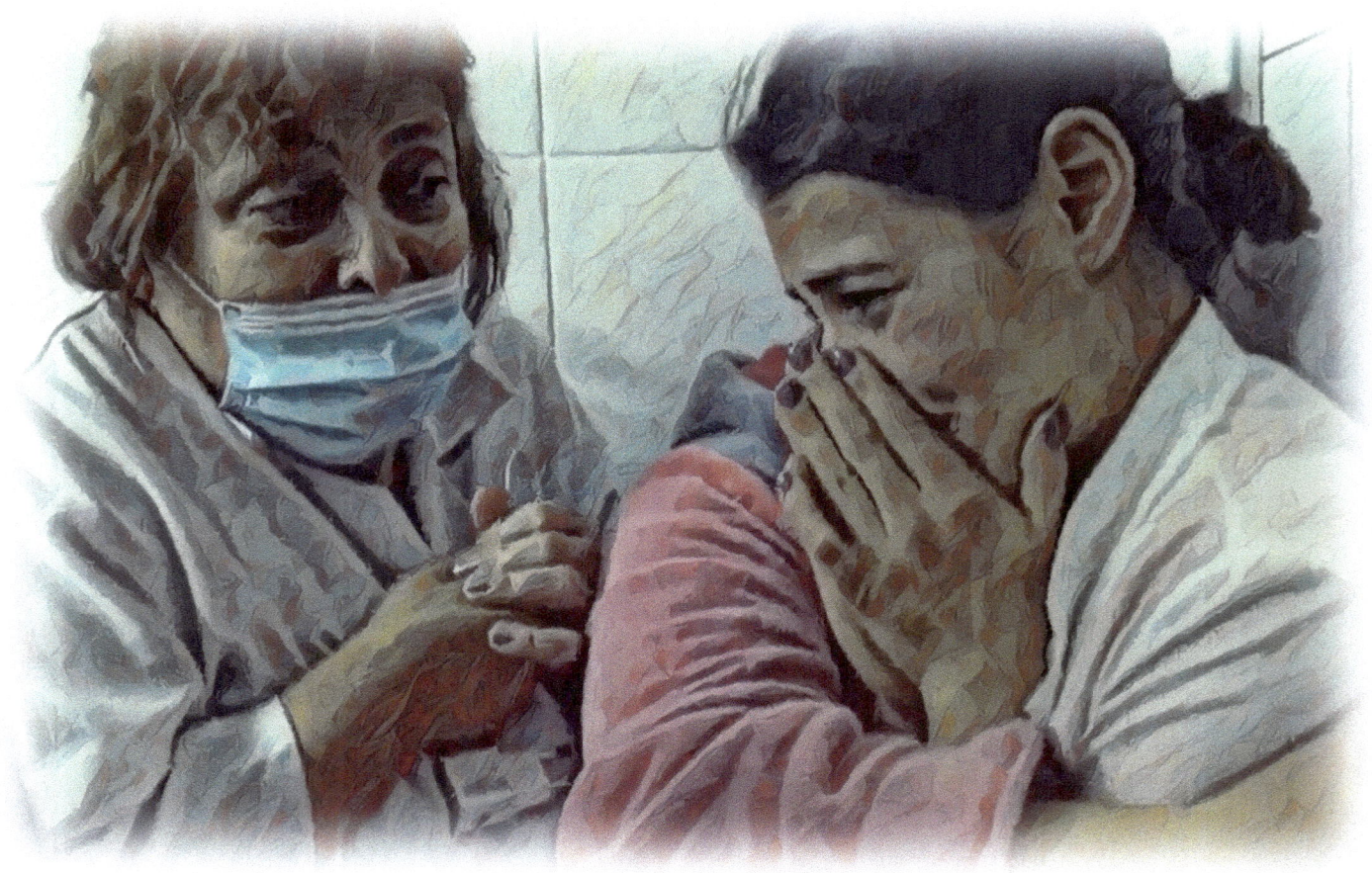

I wanted to hear from Khachents on what types of war crimes he witnessed. He shared with me, "They used, not just air weaponry, but various Naval armaments as well against our towns and villages where they bombarded and laid waste to hectares. These were peaceful, civilian areas where they attacked women and children... in reality, there were no troops stationed there... places with no military objects, positions. They were just civilian areas where people were simply living their lives."

In another BBC interview with Aliyev, the reporter asked, "Let me tell you, President Aliyev what our own BBC colleagues have seen. They were in Stepanakert in Nagorno Karabakh on 1st, 2nd, and 3rd of October. They've witnessed random shelling of a town, including an emergency services center, an apartment block destroyed. People tried to flee... there was a drone overhead. Shortly afterwards, there was more shelling nearby. They categorized it as indiscriminate shelling of a town without clear military targets. Now, this is not hearsay. This is witnessed and filmed by the BBC." How does he respond to this, you ask? "I doubt this witnessing; I doubt it." Dumbfounded, she replied, "Well, they were there, President Aliyev." He confidently replied, "So what they were there? It doesn't mean anything. That can be fake news."

She continued to say, "There is evidence that you have used cluster munitions in civilian areas in the streets of Stepanakert, documented extensively by Human Rights Watch, photographs, videos, and testimonies from witnesses, and they actually had the opportunity to go to the scene. Now, why are you using cluster munitions which can be so imprecise in a civilian area?" President Aliyev replied, "We are not using them. This is another fake news. It is Armenia that is using cluster bombs." In shock, she responded, "So everything is fake news?" and he idiotically replied, "Of course, why not?"

Exiled Azerbaijani blogger Mahammad Mirzali stabbed at least 16 times in knife attack in France

March 16, 2021 3:46 PM EDT

I had the opportunity to chat with Azerbaijani blogger Mahammad Mirzali about the situation in Artsakh. He spoke openly about his opinions on Aliyev and the Azerbaijani government. He has been exiled from Azerbaijan and was attacked by radicals in France, where he was stabbed 16 times with a knife. Thankfully he survived the attack and continues to share his thoughts on the subject.

i. Boyun-boyuna
ermiş, əllərini
oynuna qoymuş
rvadını, qızını,
ğlunu süzdü. İst-
di baltanı süra-
inin üstündən
ötürüb onları
ıpsın. Amma bax-
ı κi, özü bir sürü
ırtıcının qabağına
ılmış ayaqları
ağlı quzunu xa-
ırladır. Səbrini
ısdı:

- Ay κirvə, axı, biz sizinlə uzun illər qapıbir qonşu olmuşu
ır süfrədə çörəκ κəsmişiκ. Mənim atamın, babamın, ulu babamı
əbri bu torpaqdadır.
Erməni daha bərκdən bağırdı:
- İndiyə qədər çörəκ κəsmişiκ, indi κəsmiriκ! Sənin babalar
a bu torpaqda çox nahaq basdırılıb.
- Bizdən hansı pisliyi görmüsünüz, ay qansız?
- Siz türκsünüz, bizim düşmənimizsiniz.
- Yaxşı, κöçəriκ. İκicə gün möhlət verin...
... Şahların beynində çox fiκir dolaşdı. O, üzünü gələnlərdə
ırinə tutdu:
-Sən Suren Dilanyan deyilsən?
- Yox.

He said to me, "Everyone knows that in the history of Azerbaijan, there was never such an immoral government as the regime of Aliyev. Ilham Aliyev, carrying years of propaganda, started a war. And what was the result? A nation, which has been under propaganda for many years, went to war... when the war started in Karabakh, the situation inside of Azerbaijan was at the peak: poverty, disappointment, unemployment, people were having uncountable problems."

"In order to drive away the attention from those problems, Ilham Aliyev successfully used the 'Karabakh card.' In the Karabakh war, Turkey wanted to show its power to the world and its own people that it is a leader in the region. I think Aliyev's and Erdogan's animosity towards its neighbors is unacceptable. I hope this issue will be solved in the near future. Erdogan and Aliyev will be thrown away from power, and then there will be peace in our region."

On December 23, 2021, Azerbaijan's Ministry of Foreign Affairs requested to Google to erase, add, or alter thousands of Armenian names of cities, towns, and cultural sites in Artsakh to Azerbaijani and Albanian names in Google maps. They are seriously relentless, and it's so heartbreaking to hear that such hatred and brainwashing still exists in this day and age, with the genocides, cultural erasure, tortures, war crimes, and the injustice.
It's too much...

I felt so helpless. I needed to shift my perspective and focus on any kind of positives that I could find in this situation. I received a phone call from Arsineh stating that Mels, the soldier who went to fight alongside his brother and was taken as a POW, is on a plane returning to Armenia.

Chapter 5:
The Armenian Spirit

The family invited us back into their home, where Mels shared parts of his experience. "I was captured December 13, 2020, and I was returned October 19, 2021. I was in captivity for ten and a half months. At the start, I could not imagine nor had any idea what was going on. I was frozen. I did not think of myself but rather of my family, of their emotional state, how they would take that news. Perhaps they were aware or unaware of my capture. Perhaps they thought I was dead or that I was alive and they were waiting for me. I don't know. They are unexplainable emotions that I can't express. I mainly thought of my family: my brother, my mother, my father, and how they were going to take that news and reconcile with it."

"There were some court proceedings that took place. They sentenced me to six years in prison. Then they handed me to the military police, where they relentlessly interrogated me. We underwent different investigation processes and met with different people. In the beginning, they charged us with 'Engaging in Terrorist Activities.' They accused us of preparing explosives in Khtsapert. They said we spread fear among the civilian populace, even though we were in areas with military personnel and no civilians at all. They accused us of crossing the border without entry papers for the purpose of making weapons and, as I said before, to engage in terrorist activities."

"I started taking certain issues lightly because I realized the most important thing in life is having a loving environment and being with the ones you love. I started to appreciate my freedom, the fresh air that I breathe, the open sky above. I would especially appreciate all of that when I look up at the sky because as long as there is a sky above you, no one can limit your freedom. It was an unexplainable feeling when I hugged my brother. I don't know; it was as if this world gave me a new reason to live."

"Like a rebirth... that what I had before, since the beginning, had come to an end. Now, I plan to finish my university degree, to be accepted into a Master's program, to receive a professional education. And in the meantime, to repair our home and build my own... start a family, and at that point, God will reveal all for me."

His story gave me hope again, and I wanted to hear more from the others whom I had spoken with. Khachents shared, "For me, after the war, it was very hard because I got frostbite, which kept me from creating new music, songs, lyrics, etc. But over time, I realized all the medicine and remedies don't work. The only cure is your devotion to your profession. After returning from the war, where I served for five extra days, upon seeing the Shushi fortress and mountains, I promised myself that I needed to be victorious in my profession because, in reality, I did not concede there."

"At present, I've conceded that I lost my friends and a piece of our Fatherland, but I feel accountable and obligated to live my life in a way that I will be worthy of my friends' sacrifice and to work in such a way where I can take my music to my Fatherland where I was born and raised and thrived... and if that longing is to be put to music, then I can use that longing to knock on the doors of hearts and say I miss it, my heart aches too, and my longing, my pain, my love, will all be put to song and through that song, I will reach people."

Mr. Phillips shared some hope with me as well; he stated, "So the U.S. has changed its attitude towards Turkey. Turkey's purchase of S-400 missiles from Russia violates the Countering American Advisories Through Sanctions Act. There is also now, in both the Senate and the House, a shared understanding that what happened at the turn of the century represents genocide and that the recent events in Artsakh are a second genocide. And I would use that term copiously in describing what happened."

Mr. Papian told me, "Politically, the Armenian Genocide is already recognized by the majority of countries. The main powers recognize it, and the last and important one was the United States. We are hoping that Great Britain and the U.K. will do this within this year as well."

The silver lining to this dark and difficult chapter was that the goal of annihilating the Armenian people not only failed but lit a fire in the diaspora. Many non-profits were formed this past year to help the people of Artsakh and Armenia, such as the Armenian Hero Project, Armenian Unity Project, Miaseen, and The Center for Truth and Justice.

I spoke with the Honorable Judge Gassia Apkarian to follow up on what CFTJ has accomplished since its inception and she stated, "The organization is about a year and a month old... we have over 200 testimonials, and based on that testimonial evidence, we have prepared two White Papers specifically related to POWs and how Azerbaijan was treating POWs... that they don't even call them POWs; they call them terrorists... the mistreatment and the torture, that was the first White Paper we submitted to Congress. The second White Paper was about how Azerbaijan was hiding POWs and denying that they had Armenians in custody."

Given all the atrocities and horrors the Armenian people have faced, they continue to fight, help one another, share their culture and support each other. I've never been prouder to be an Armenian than I am right now. I wanted to hear what being an Armenian means from my peers. Mels shared, "To be an Armenian is to have that love of your culture instilled from the start because you were born an Armenian; you have to be able to protect that name, that dignity, all of it."

Mr. Hacopian stated, "It means one thing, resurrection. Every successful country tells a narrative about us, and for 100 years, we've told the wrong narrative. What's important about us is not the crucifixion; it's the resurrection."

The Honorable Judge Gassia Apkarian said, "Being Armenian means you have to stay Armenian. To stay Armenian, you have to fight to stay Armenian. And fighting to stay Armenian makes it a cause for me."

Khachents shared, "To be an Armenian isn't a choice, a destiny, or luck. Being an Armenian is the most trying and heaviest burden to shoulder in the world. Being an Armenian means fighting against this injustice alone, like we did in the past wars. It means to never surrender and to understand that your forefathers, the 'freedom fighter' spirit, your fathers and grandfather's spirits all fight alongside you to the grave. Your forefathers constantly remind you that you have your unique story, and you must preserve that."

"You have religion and faith... and your people underwent the longest and cruelest of genocides, along with victories from wars. And it is your duty to honor that sacrifice by planting yourself in your fatherland like a tree."

To me, being an Armenian means to be resilient and having a spirit that is unbreakable. That is the Armenian Spirit.

"I should like to see any power of the world destroy this race, this small tribe of unimportant people, whose wars have all been fought and lost, whose structures have crumbled, literature unread, music is unheard, and prayers are no more answered. Go ahead, destroy Armenia. See if you can do it. Send them into the desert without bread or water. Burn their homes and churches. Then see if they will not laugh, sing and pray again. For when two of them meet anywhere in the world, see if they will not create a new Armenia." – William Saroyan.

In Loving Memory of

Garnik Khlghatyan
July 28, 2001 – September 27, 2020

If you would like to get involved and help support, please check out:

www.CFTJustice.org

www.Miaseen.org

@ArmenianUnityProject

@ArmenianHeroProject

@GuardianEagles

www.AngelaAsatrian.com

Special Thank You:

Alex Asatrian
Allen Davityan
Nicholas Davityan
Joseph Davityan
Elaina Mnatsakanian
Ryan Mnatsakanian
Honorable Judge Gassia Apkarian
Arthur Khachents
Fatma Muge Gocek
David L. Phillips
Jacob Pursley, Ph.D.
Uzay Bulut
Mirzali Mahammad
Ara Papian
Rouben Galichian
Maggie Arutyunyan, Esq.
Arsineh Arakel, Esq.
Gevork Nazaryan
T's Catering
Diamondized Group
Tahmasian Media Marketing
Talar Keoseyan
Brittany Lynn Page